MULTI-PASSIONATE

How to Claim Your Identity & Radiate as a Multi Passionate in a Linear World

Sigute Zitikyte

Sigute Publishing

Contents

Being multi-passionate is your superpower ix

Permission to be you 1
Embrace your multi-passionate heart 3
Claim your identity 5
Face the resistance 7
The pleasure of sustainable success 9
Build trust in your future self 11
Drop your grip on perfectionism 13
Release your idea into the real world 15
Manage your mind 17
Stop trying to save everyone 19
Honour your boundaries 21
Hold high standards 23
Indulge in calmness 25
Romance your intuition 27
Life is art 29
Creativity is a verb 31
Learn to change your mind 33
Have the courage to quit 35
Speak your identity into existence 37
Attract your soul people 39
final reminders... 41
Embrace reinvention 42
Don't indulge in the overwhelm 44
Start today 46
Be proudly multi-passionate 48

About the Author 53

For the ambitious, multi-passionate,
perfectionist, and overachieving professional
who dreams of more than the status quo...

in other words, for you & me

*"Don't live the same year 75 times
and call it a life."*

Robin Sharma

Being multi-passionate is your superpower

Some labels can act as a crutch (like "introvert", which wonderfully charismatic people sometimes hide behind). Other labels are more like a podium, helping you stand taller.

Adopting the label of "*multi-passionate*" has given me permission to claim my *full* identity.

You see, I've always been driven, curious, and ambitious. But I've also carried shame about not having found my "one thing". That little thought used to dangle over any success I would achieve, or any goal I would conquer, or any new passions I would dive into. Always at the ready to remind me that "real" success is going all in on *one thing*.

How could I not carry this shame? Traditional success, after all, is measured by the amount of life we're willing to sacrifice. The further we climb the ladder, the smaller and smaller we become as we sacrifice parts of ourselves with each step up.

Perhaps this works for some. But for me? I knew it never would.

So I re-defined success for myself as a measure of how *expansive* I could make my life.

I built a career that evolved with my never-ending quest for personal growth.

And I gave myself permission to embrace my multi-passionate self in a world that often feels like it only wants to see one dimension of me.

The tools I share in this book have been my devoted allies in supporting my journey and I hope they will do the same for you in yours. You belong with us, the multi-passionates, in our fabulous underground world where *loving life* is the mission. We are ordinary people living extraordinary lives. We find joy in the simple luxuries of life and we don't get sucked into the noise of the world. We love our careers. We love our relationships. We love to travel the world. We love to soak up the richness of our lives.

I'm so happy you joined us. And I hope this book becomes your oasis when the world tries to knock you off your multi-passionate throne.

— Sigute Zitikyte

Permission to be you

"Instead of being authentic with the person society has painted of you, try being authentic with the person you are painting yourself to be."

Inside of you lives a version of yourself that is waiting to be released: the visionary founder, the respected thought leader, the bestselling author, the charismatic speaker, or maybe the passionate change-maker.

You learned how to play the game of *traditional* success and now you're ready to build towards *authentic* success. You're ready to shed a lifetime of rule following, of being a cog in the machine of society.

To do this, you have to unlearn following your *ego* and relearn following your *intuition*. You have to choose to give up the default setting of a mediocre life and upgrade your life settings with the details that make it exquisite... *for you*.

Your life is not meant to be explained. It's meant to be experienced.

And the more we concern ourselves with trying to explain it, trying to make it palatable for everyone around us, that's when we lose the plot: that life is art. Nothing more than brushstrokes on a white canvas—not a single one less beautiful than another.

We stumble into this realization at one point or another—lucky for you, you're already here!

Your perspective of life has changed and now you're standing at a crossroads: do I venture forward as my most authentic and exquisite self or do I go back to a mediocre life? We both know the answer. And this book will help you keep taking one step in front of the other.

It's time to stop questioning your desires.

It's time to stop questioning your ambition.

It's time to stop questioning your vision for success.

It's time to finally embrace *your multi-passionate heart.*

Embrace your multi-passionate heart

"To escape mediocrity, you have to invent your own identity in the world."

M*ulti-passionate* is a term that describes a way of life that's filled with unlimited freedom to *be* you, *do* you, and continue discovering the *new* you.

It's a life-long commitment to pursue your curiosities and have the patience and trust to see how they'll connect into a beautiful life path that's uniquely yours. In other words, it's a journey of doing things that feel random while trusting that your future self will make the most of those random things.

It's a vote towards trusting your intuition and relinquishing control of the need to fit into a perfect little box with a perfect little bow.

You are not a widget.

You, my friend, are a glittering diamond that can't help but radiate in a million directions.

You didn't stumble into this life to do the same thing every day based on a proven formula that's guaranteed to never change. That kind of life is based on fear. And fear is boring. It's mediocre. It's missing colour and laughter. It's a gradual loss of excitement, joy, and *joie de vivre.*

Your multi-passionate heart is your knight in shining armour that's here to save you from that version of life. How lucky are you to have it?!

If you listen to it, it will guide you to building a life and career that is forever expressing your full potential. And that's your real journey in this lifetime—*to claim your identity.*

Claim your identity

"Nothing scares society more than a person who has claimed themselves."

Most people live their entire lives at the mercy of who the world shaped them to be.

Instead of taking the reins on reshaping themselves into their dream self, they longingly wish for a perfect childhood that might have guaranteed them a dream life.

But that's not how it works—there is no perfect incubator that will guide us humans towards our fullest expression. That's why wishing for a different past is a pointless pursuit—because a perfect past is not what creates a fully expressed future.

Transforming your *current* identity into your *chosen* identity is how an exquisite life is built.

This is your life, not a community project. You do not have to conform to anything. In fact, it's the people who are suffering from conforming to the rules who are the most resentful when others break free of them.

It's here that your multi-passionate heart will get its first taste of resistance from those trapped in a linear life.

Don't shrink from it or let it take you off your quest for an exquisite life.

You must learn to *face the resistance.*

Face the resistance

"Choosing to be a joyful and confident person is an act of rebellion in a world that finds it easier to love a suffering person."

"How dare you dream of a better world when the current one is up in flames!" is what you may hear when others get a whiff of your desire for more.

There's a reason why misery loves company—in times of fear and darkness, we don't want to be alone. We want company. And the quickest way to find company? Through shared misery. But misery is a weak bond that will never fill your cup. It only creates a false sense of connection—leaving you even more disconnected than before. It's a cage for those who have forgotten that the world is abundant, that your intuition is always willing to guide you, and that opportunities are always present... they simply need to be noticed and claimed.

It's an act of rebellion to refuse to sit in communal misery.

It's an act of rebellion to have a strong vision and build a supportive environment.

Embrace this life of a rebel!

Cultivate your abundance mindset. It will be your shield against the dark forces. Do not settle for the scarcity mindset you were conditioned to have. (*Wouldn't that be convenient for those desiring to have you play small!*) Do not cling to one job, one skill, one version of life based on a fear of letting go and having nothing. Do not cling to the false sense of belonging in a community that doesn't value your unique gifts.

There is another way to live life. It is the way of the multi-passionate who claims their identity.

The following pages will help you sharpen your new superpower.

The pleasure of sustainable success

Most of us have been conditioned to optimize our lives for *speed...*

How fast can you climb the corporate ladder? How quickly can you become a millionaire? How soon can you buy your forever home? How early can you arrive at your picture-perfect life where unicorns prance around your living room?

If you're looking for a shortcut, you'll find plenty... but your search for quick success will only benefit those selling it to you. Avoid the traps that come with optimizing your life for *speed* by optimizing your life for *pleasure*.

The pleasure of trusting yourself and not worrying what others think.

The pleasure of releasing a tight grip on life.

The pleasure of being a disciplined person who takes consistent action.

The pleasure of managing your mind and not being triggered easily.

The pleasure of fully immersing yourself into your desires.

The pleasure of protecting your vision with strong boundaries.

The pleasure of having high standards.

The pleasure of a slow life.

The pleasure of being guided by your intuition.

The pleasure of living an unscripted life.

The pleasure of unleashing your creativity.

The pleasure of growth and change.

The pleasure of quitting what no longer serves you.

The pleasure of being your authentic self.

The pleasure of being surrounded by your soul people.

...When there's so much pleasure to be experienced in life, how could anyone want speed?

Build trust in your future self

When you start to feel overwhelmed, try telling yourself: "My overthinking brain is really active right now."

It's impossible to claim your identity and radiate as your authentic self until you can build trust in your future self to have your back... no matter what.

It's the complete opposite of a simple life where you have the luxury of time and space to build 100% confidence before taking action. Up until this point, you could see what was ahead of you, slow your life down to get all your ducks in a row, and only *then* take action in perfect conditions. Every disagreement was accounted for, every obstacle was mitigated, and with that—a mediocre life was born.

But you're not after a mediocre life, so it's time to change how you operate in the world.

Building trust in yourself looks like accepting an offer before you feel ready, committing to a new project without knowing how you'll accomplish it, following a new curiosity even when it feels random, and saying "yes" when it still feels terrifying.

Most importantly, it's getting comfortable with saying "I don't know" to someone who asks why you are doing something. Because in your heart, that "I don't know" is followed by "and yet, I trust my future self to figure it out."

If you want to live an exquisite life, build trust in your future self.

Drop your grip on perfectionism

When you start to feel like you're not good enough, try telling yourself: "My inner child doesn't feel safe right now."

Perfectionism is a sneaky bugger because it looks and sounds noble, but it's an admission that you have shame about who you are and how you are showing up in this world. It's an admission that you don't feel good or smart enough.

There is no universal standard for being a perfect human, nor are there standards for being a perfect friend or parent or employee or entrepreneur or creative. There are only impossible standards that we create for ourselves to stay in a cycle of shame. Why? Because at some point, we decided that *shame* is what keeps us from becoming useless and deplorable wastes of space...

You didn't get this far in life *because* of your perfectionism.

You got this far *despite* your perfectionism.

Now think how much further you could go without carrying the weight of shame?

As you release your need for control, you will find that a multi-passionate life will begin to naturally unravel in front of you. You will begin to feel safe in the knowing that life is not meant to be figured out, but to be lived. You will begin to let your guard down and step into your soft era where pleasure and calmness and slowness are allowed back in.

As anyone who has conquered perfectionism knows, dropping the tight grip over your life doesn't turn you into a failure.

It unleashes your radiance.

Release your idea into the real world

When you start to feel resistance, try telling yourself: "My overthinking brain doesn't run the show."

It's hard to build an exquisite life when you're constantly overthinking your ideas, questioning if you've gone crazy, and wondering if perhaps a mediocre life is *"as good as it's gonna get"* for you.

But the world behaves differently when you decide to take action. It immediately swoops in and rewards you for birthing a new idea into existence. It will give you everything you need to survive that labour. It's meant to feel hard, it's meant to feel overwhelming—those are signs you're breaking an invisible shield that exists between your mind and the real world.

You will feel the most resistance right before an idea bursts into the world...

How many times have you backed out at this point?

Avoiding the release of your ideas into the world is the start of a tumultuous relationship with your ambition... and a lifetime of stop-and-go for your vision. You will fill your day with empty planning that keeps you stuck in burnout, without any results to show for it.

Release *the thing* and your efforts will be worth it! With each release, your hesitation grows shorter. The more you release, the more your momentum builds.

It's why multi-passionates have momentum on their side for achieving wild goals that don't make sense in a linear world.

Whatever you do, *release the thing.*

Manage your mind

When you start to feel like you're broken, try telling yourself: "I've been trained to doubt myself because then I'm easier to control."

Every ambitious professional already has a side hustle...

It's called doubting themselves.

Do you really think there's a title or rank you will reach where your self-worth, self-trust, and self-love are just sitting and waiting for you? Those things can never be the reward because how you feel on the *way up* is exactly how you will feel when you *arrive*.

Thoughts are a muscle and the more you think a thought, the stronger it becomes in your mind. And a thought, just like a muscle, doesn't just appear because you walked into a new room—even if that room is the most fabulous and luxurious room you've ever stepped into.

Your shitty thoughts have also walked into that room alongside you.

The linear world was built on hierarchy (*so you always feel behind*), on competition (*so you never slow down*), and on rules (*so you stop trusting your intuition*). Nothing has gone wrong if you feel doubt, shame, or not good enough. In fact, the system is working flawlessly! The goal is to remove joy, creativity, and the desire to build an exquisite life from your mind. Why? Because an abundant mind can never be manipulated by scarcity-fuelled power.

When your mind is filled with doubt, it's no wonder you might not want to add new pursuits or goals to your life. It's hard to imagine being incredibly great at 50 different things when your self-doubt is hoarding 49 of those spots, limiting your potential to just doing *one thing*.

The more doubt and shame you can remove from your mind, the more passion and pursuits you can fill it with.

It's for this reason that your ability to manage your mind is a prerequisite for your multi-passionate life.

Stop trying to save everyone

When you start to feel selfish, try telling yourself: "My people pleasing is eager for attention today."

I know you well, my dear people pleaser.

You will take this permission to be multi-passionate and you will channel it towards doing *even more* for others.

Here's the thing. Being multi-passionate is about doing more things that *you* are passionate about, not more things that your sense of obligation and responsibility are requesting of you. You can't spend your whole life hunkered down in a state of exhaustion and burnout because you're on a mission to single-handedly save the world.

How arrogant of us to think we are here to save everyone else!

You will never experience more freedom than when you realize that everyone—including *you!*— is on their own journey and all we can do is inspire each other to stay the course.

As you are claiming your identity for yourself, everyone else is on their own journey of claiming *their* identity for *themselves.*

Isn't that a relief?

Isn't it great news that you being burnt out will never save the world?

Isn't it wonderful that you can prioritize your passions and trust that others can also choose to prioritize theirs?

Honour your boundaries

When you start to feel pulled in many directions, try telling yourself: "I am the protector of my life's vision."

You don't need help prioritizing your passions, you need help saying *no* to your non-passions.

The most magnetic force on the planet, beyond gravity, is a strong vision for the life you want to live. It will pull opportunities and people and experiences your way.

And if you don't have a strong vision for yourself, you will feel the pull of other people's grand visions. Without one of your own, you will feel this unshakeable urge to help them achieve theirs. That's not necessarily a bad thing, especially in small doses, but it becomes problematic when you allow that magnetic pull to tear you away from the life you are building for yourself.

Don't blame others for having magnetic visions. Get curious about how you can build one of your own.

Remember, vision respects vision. When you see someone in their power, claiming their identity, pursuing their goals, fanning the flame of their big vision, you won't be able to stop yourself from admiring them because you recognize the effort it takes to play this game.

Others with visions feel the same way looking at you, so never stop building your boundaries! Those in the arena will admire you for them and those who have a problem with your boundaries will one day understand how much they failed to recognize your radiant potential.

Until then, focus on your vision and prioritize *your* passions.

Hold high standards

When you start to feel like you're too much, try telling yourself: "My self-love will show others how to love themselves."

Not everyone will want to join you on your multi-passionate journey.

Remember, this is a path for those willing to put in the *effort* of claiming their identity.

And since most won't join you, it can be said that most will want you to stay as you are. You'll find yourself wasting precious time explaining and defending yourself instead of building your desired reality.

Create a red velvet rope policy in your life for the people, places, conversations, experiences, and thoughts you allow into your inner circle. Adopt high standards as soon as possible!

The reality is, no environment is perfect and each one can lead you astray from who you are. It's not so much about finding the perfect environment to settle into, but about intentionally collecting new experiences and interactions that will fuel you to continue raising your standards and expectations of life.

Your mission is to never give up on your deep love of life because of the opinions of those who lost theirs long ago...

Hold onto your high standards. Especially in a world that has settled for a cheap, fast, easy, and uninspired way of living.

Indulge in calmness

When you start to feel like you're lazy, try telling yourself: "My energy is a resource I choose to replenish."

It's never about *what* you do, it's about *how* you do it.

Building a multi-passionate life requires a strong practice of choosing calmness as your "*how*" and ditching the anxious *clawing-your-way-to-the-finish-line* approach.

There's a stereotype for success. That it's loud, brash, dominating, and on the front page news around the world.

But that's a very limited view of success. While it might be the talked about style of success, it's not the most *enjoyed* style of success. How could it be when it's a life filled with clutter, noise, and burnout?

Calmness is the antidote to burnout. It's the ability to move with quiet confidence towards your desires and towards building your exquisite life.

While others are running, you are striding.

While others are frantic, you are graceful.

While others are burnt out, you are *just beginning*.

Romance your intuition

When you start to feel behind in life, try telling yourself: "Societal norms are trying to get inside my brain today."

void becoming the person who constantly asks:

"What should I do? Just tell me *what* to do!"

"How should I do it? Just tell me *how* to do it!"

These questions are a hint that you may be letting the outside world rule your inner kingdom and run your life. The more you ask these questions the more variety of answers you'll get—slowly spiralling into a place of doom and dread.

There is another way...

Your intuition—or what artists often call *the muse*—speaks in whispers. She wants to know you are listening before she shares her magic with you. She wants to see you are devoted before she reveals herself. She wants to feel your commitment before she shares her deepest desires. It is an honour to hear your intuition's whispers.

There is no cookie cutter formula for your unique blend of desires. Not only that, but you are evolving so often—and in unpredictable ways—that you will be spinning your wheels at each turn.

Create space to connect with *you*. Start asking a new set of questions. This time, to yourself.

Who are your soul people?

Why are you passionate about them?

How can you be of service to them?

Life is art

When you start to feel like you're doing life wrong, try telling yourself: "My conditioning has a strong grip on me today."

Claiming your identity in a world that won't stop changing is nothing short of *necessary*. It's a vote on *you* as the creator of your own future.

Most people would rather choose suffering if it's by a known evil than risk building a life they love—one that's in their control—if it comes with the potential risk of a setback they don't yet know.

Success can be achieved in a million different ways and anyone who argues that it can only be achieved one of three ways is ignoring the changing world. Or rather, they have buried their heads below the sand—a coping mechanism to resist change and maintain a sense of safety.

Do not argue with them. Let them take their own journey of embracing change. Ignore their demands that you must "*pick one thing!*" or "*settle down!*".

Being realistic is gaslighting for a heart that wants a more expansive life. Just because they stuffed themselves into a little box of potential doesn't mean you have to.

Doing one thing doesn't create success. Being so jazzed up about your life and your career is what makes you radiate so bright that you become a magnet for opportunities.

There is no "success police" that will tell you you're doing life wrong. There is no "passion police" that will tell you how your passions and paycheck need to be balanced.

Life is art. There are no rules. You are a canvas that either you paint or the world paints.

Grab that paintbrush back. Choose your colours. And start painting.

Creativity is a verb

When you start to feel like you're not creative, try telling yourself: "My self-expression is struggling to show up today."

"I'm not creative" is a lie that every ambitious professional has told themselves at one point in their lives—maybe even still today?

We get split into two camps very early on: we're either the creative kid or the smart kid.

And then we get pushed into one of those sides and spend the rest of our lives judging the "lesser" part of ourselves.

What if we were raised *whole*?

What if creativity and smarts were verbs, not labels we stick to our foreheads?

A multi-passionate life is a vote towards becoming a *whole* person again. That's what makes it a superpower—you become doubly powerful. It's time to show love to the "lesser" side of you that got no sunlight. Coax them out. Play their favourite game, do their favourite art. Show them that a messy, colourful, creative life can feel safe.

The linear world thrives when people repress their creativity because it leads to self-expression. And self-expression leads to self-awareness.

And self-awareness? It leads to reclaiming your identity and radiating as your authentic self.

If you don't feel creative, all you have to do is start creating...

Anything.

Learn to change your mind

When you start to feel like you're all over the place, try telling yourself: "My ego is very active today."

When you're exploring a new trail, you have the freedom to change your mind. To take two steps forward, one step back, three to the left, and then two to the right.

Only when a trail is a single lane, moving in one direction, does it feel odd to change directions. So it's understandable that our conditioning to follow a linear path also comes with conditioning to avoid changing our minds.

We don't want to look like the weirdo who stops mid-sidewalk to turn around.

But as a multi-passionate explorer? You will explore many directions, hold contradicting ideas in the palms of your hands, and live a life that's filled with picking up passions, reflecting on them, and setting them back down.

This is not a flaw, it's your intuitive process. And the ability to change your mind—without triggering a defensive reaction from your ego—is important to cultivate.

A fragile ego is quick to save face. It wants to look smart and successful. It wants to look powerful and in control. It wants to float regally on top of the water, despite how frantically its feet are moving below.

Become impenetrable to the idea that you have to follow through on every passion.

After all, who would you rather be?

Someone who has 50 ideas and "only" follows through on 15 of them?

Or someone who only has two ideas and follows through on both of them?

Go on, change your mind.

Have the courage to quit

When you start to feel like you're not committed, try telling yourself: "My identity is ready to evolve."

The difference between being someone who is overwhelmed with too many things on their plate and someone who is empowered as a multi-passionate is *your courage to quit.*

Get comfortable with the cycle of adding new things and dropping old ones. Don't be afraid to give up the good to go for the great.

But in a society that celebrates "sticking with it", you might find yourself wanting to stay with the choices you've outgrown instead of risking disappointing others with your evolution. It's a people pleaser's worst nightmare...

Just remember that the real disservice is staying in an environment where you've lost your radiance. The value of our passions isn't how long we cling onto them, it's how expansive they make our lives.

Squeeze as much as you can out of each passion, each pursuit, each curiosity...

And then release it.

One of the most beautiful lessons is understanding that everything in life—the people, places, and experiences—either come to you for a season, a reason, or a lifetime.

Allow for the natural cycles of life to play out.

No clingy energy, please.

Speak your identity into existence

When you start to feel conceited, try telling yourself: "My purpose is to invite others to experience my authentic self."

Most entrepreneurs will say that entrepreneurship changed their life—that it was entrepreneurship that finally forced them into the driver's seat of their life.

But if you dig a little deeper, get a little more nuanced with that shift, you notice that perhaps it was them finally using their voice and expressing their personal brand that made entrepreneurship transformational.

That's what makes personal branding—or the art of *speaking your identity into existence*—the ultimate personal development journey. The process of defining what you stand for, what your mission is, and stepping into your full personal power is what radically changes your life.

Why is this nuance so important to make?

Because you don't have to be an entrepreneur to start unlocking your personal power.

Your authentic self—the one that doesn't fit into a box—deserves to be shared.

And you have the power to start sharing.

Attract your soul people

When you start to feel alone, try telling yourself:
"My fear of rejection is looking for attention today."

Claiming your identity won't happen if you're surrounded by people who make you feel shame about who you are.

Go where you are celebrated, not where you are tolerated.

Cultivating your environment with your soul people is a key part of the process to embracing who you are and bringing even more of yourself to the surface.

Be *over the top.*

Be *too much.*

Be *extra.*

You must get intentional about finding and attracting your soul people. One of the best ways to do this is to stand up and wave your freak flag so they can spot you in the crowd! How else will they know that you also speak their language of *excitement for your shared passion*? How else will they know that you also see the world in the *same colours as them*?

If you take the first step in expressing who you are, your soul people will be able to recognize you and join the path you're walking. There's no better feeling than choosing an empty path in life and watching it grow from just you as the lone ranger to you and your soul people striding along together.

But to do that... you have to swallow your pride, swallow your nerves, and start walking down that path alone. But I promise, the momentary blip of time where you are walking alone and feeling exposed is worth it. No risk driven by the heart is ever futile. When you act from love, from connection, from emotion, you glow differently. You have an invisible shield around you that gives you an extra *oomph* of radiance to light up a dark sky.

Your soul people are waiting for you. Don't leave them hanging.

final reminders...

Embrace reinvention

You came here to take a big juicy bite out of life and experience all that it has to offer—the happiness, the sadness, the mountains, the ocean, the love, the hurt, the storms, the flowers, the grief, the gratitude, the joy, the fear.

There is no *arriving* for you.

The only constant about you is the hum of your ambition. Follow it. You don't need to know how you're going to get there, or how it should look, or what the "right" way is, you simply need to know where you are going.

Have a crystal clear vision of what you want to accomplish. Trust me, *you know*. Get clear on the lifestyle and experiences you desire.

Yes, you deserve them! *All* of them!

If you focus too much on what your life looks like from the outside—questioning if you're reinventing too much, changing your mind too often, if people are confused about your actions, or judging your pivots yet again—then you will never move. You will stay paralyzed, scared of stirring up attention, yet again. But is it really worth letting your mind sabotage your growth?

The only people who do not reinvent are the ones who aren't growing. If you love to learn and grow, build a life that reflects that, not hides it!

You must be willing to tolerate discomfort and a little chaos in your life. Loosen your grip on your life and your image—allow your radiance to shine through. It speaks louder than words.

For now, follow your excitement.

Don't indulge in the overwhelm

The weight of a big vision is heavy. Allowing yourself to see your potential is painful. It forces you to face your shortcomings. It's why building an exquisite life stirs up a flurry of negative thoughts. It's like a snowglobe—every time you step outside your comfort zone, it's like you've flipped the snowglobe of your life upside down. Sit back and observe the explosion of sparkles all around you.

Nothing has gone wrong. You simply shook up the snowglobe.

Overwhelm will make you think something has gone wrong. It will grab at everything around you and present it to you as proof of its validity. It will say, "*Yes you do have too much going on! And yes you don't need to fill your life with unwanted stress! And of course you deserve a break right now. And yes, this is all a stupid idea!*"

Don't indulge in these "facts" your overwhelm is presenting to you. What if you actually have too *little* going on? What if filling your life with *more* healthy stress is good for you? What if taking a break will make you feel more *drained*? What if *all of life* is a stupid idea and we're making the most of it?

Start to familiarize yourself with the little snowflakes that show up inside your snowglobe. What do they say? It's always the same—the thing with our negative thoughts is they're not very creative. It's the same old stories that come up each time.

They simply want to be acknowledged, so greet them when they arrive, marvel at how intricately they dance with one another—let out an "*Oooh! Aaah!*"—then thank them for their majestic show and get back to business.

Start today

There is a certain ease to living a linear life... a simplicity to it...

That's why falling into a mediocre life is so easy—it takes no effort to follow in someone else's footsteps. It's a path that doesn't stir up your snowglobe of emotions and which fits perfectly into the idea we've sold that we should strive to "*just be happy!*"

In other words, we're told to avoid feeling our full rainbow of emotions, only the socially approved ones. How typical of us hierarchy-loving humans to yet again find ourselves ranking emotions as "good" and "bad".

In a multi-passionate life, we don't strive to be *just* happy. We strive to feel *alive*.

And if *aliveness* is the goal, then *perfection* is our sign we're off course.

Forget the idea that your life can be mapped out on a piece of paper. Perhaps that's how you've operated until now, getting through each day, each year, knowing exactly what's around the corner. This is the fastest way to drain your excitement for life and empty your tank for action... resulting in a life that looks perfect, but feels dead inside.

Resist the urge to map it all. Only those on a predefined path can predict the speed and direction of their actions. By definition, pursuing a multi-passionate life entails charting your own course. That's what feeling *alive* entails.

The productivity machine inside our brain is programmed to believe that taking massive action each day is what's required of us, that a moment of relaxation will crumble everything we've built until now. That kind of thinking is steeped in scarcity... something the linear world thrives on.

But when you are walking your own path? Taking a few giant steps and then pausing to enjoy the view is finally possible.

Start today. A short 30 minutes of uncomfortable action is all you need.

Then take a pause and smell the roses.

Be proudly multi-passionate

There is no label that has given me more freedom and abundance than the label of "multi-passionate".

It has given me clarity in who I am—paradoxically, by embracing the uncertainty and wildness of life.

It has allowed me to claim my true identity and continue to evolve into my future self.

Being multi-passionate is an act of rebellion as it mimics nature's wild, impulsive, and unpredictable energy, which cannot be controlled or explained by the linear world. It's a way of life that connects you to your inner genius and creates quantum leaps that disrupt a structured and logical society.

Your life is not meant to be explained... only things in small boxes can be dissected and explained.

You are meant to be experienced... from every corner and every facet of who you are!

And as you step into your most authentic self, you will inspire those around you to do the same. Creating a world that's rich in diversity, uniqueness, and *exquisiteness*.

"There's only one very good life and that's the life you know you want and you make it yourself."

Diana Vreeland

About the Author

Sigute Zitikyte is a speaker, writer, and coach who believes that being multi-passionate is your superpower. She writes a weekly column that inspires ambitious professionals to connect with their intuition, use their voice, and start building a career off the beaten path.

To learn more, visit:

www.sigutezitikyte.com

instagram.com/sigutezitikyte

Manufactured by Amazon.ca
Bolton, ON

33898558R00037